# CREATIVE JOURNEY
## THE ART OF DISCOVERY

*"O beautiful for spacious skies,*
*For amber waves of grain,*
*For purple mountain majesties*
*Above the fruited plain!*
*America! America!*
*God shed His grace on thee*
*And crown thy good with brotherhood*
*From sea to shining sea!"*

- "America the Beautiful" by Katharine Lee Bates

Join me on an artistic journey through the 50 states of America, as we explore the wonders that inspired these timeless words. Let us marvel at the grandeur of America's diverse national parks, the majestic mountains, the serene forests, and the power of the endless rivers and waterfalls that grace these lands. From sea to shining sea, let us discover together the breathtaking beauty that is America.

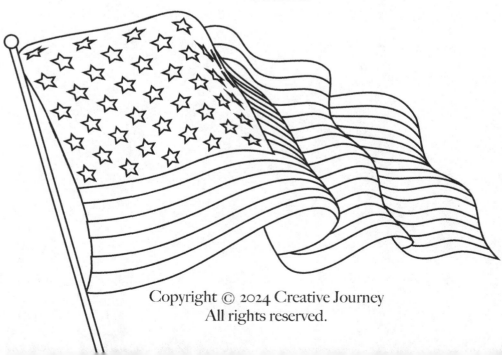

# Alabama
## Conecuh National Forest

The Conecuh National Forest in Alabama is home to one of the last remaining populations of the endangered red-cockaded woodpecker, a species known for its cooperative breeding behavior and its reliance on longleaf pine forests for nesting.

# Alaska
## Denali National Park

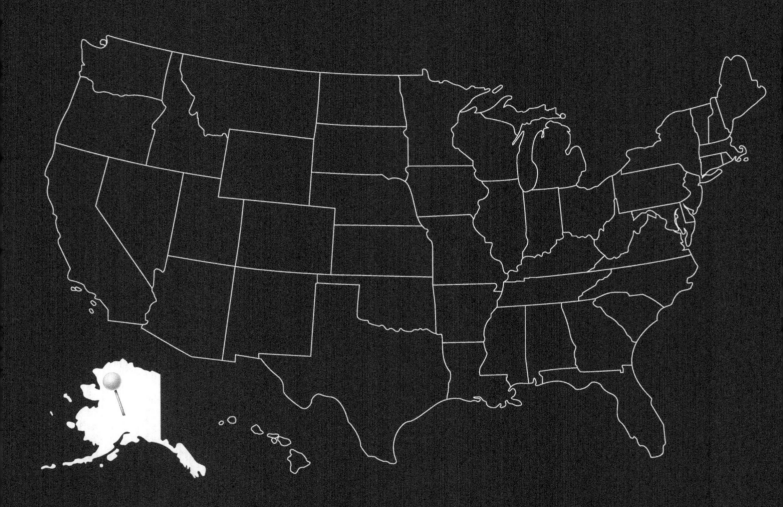

Denali National Park is home to North America's tallest peak, Denali (formerly Mount McKinley), towering at 20,310 feet above sea level. Interestingly, the mountain's summit is so high that it creates its own weather, often shrouding it in clouds even on clear days.

# Arizona
## Saguaro National Park

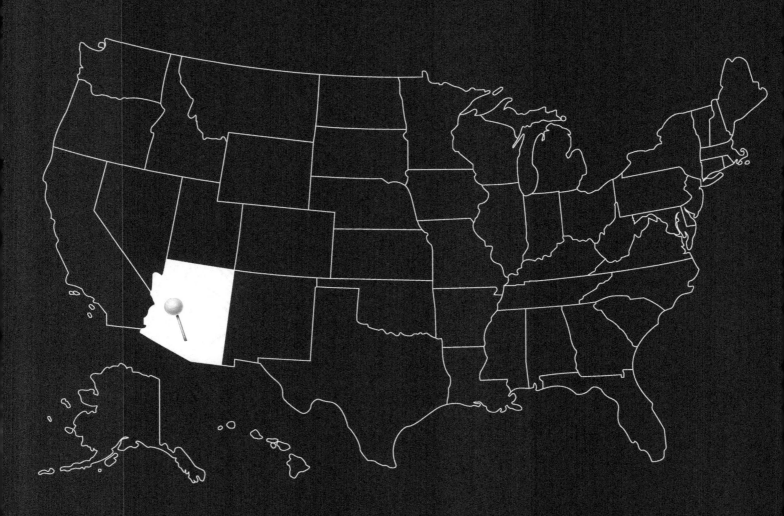

Saguaro National Park in Arizona is the only place in the world where the iconic saguaro cactus grows naturally. These towering cacti, which can reach up to 40 feet in height, can live for more than 150 years and are a symbol of the American Southwest.

# Arkansas
## Hot Springs National Park

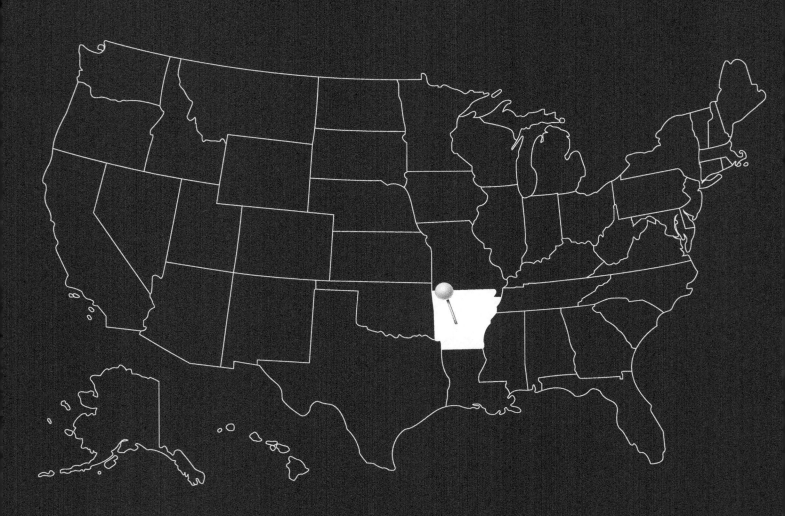

Hot Springs National Park is home to natural thermal springs that produce an average of 700,000 gallons of hot water per day. These hot springs have been used for therapeutic purposes for centuries and are protected within the park.

# California
## Big Sur

Big Sur is renowned for its stunning and rugged coastline along Highway 1, considered one of the most scenic drives in the world. The highway winds along sheer cliffs, offering breathtaking views of the Pacific Ocean below.

# Colorado
## Rocky Mountains

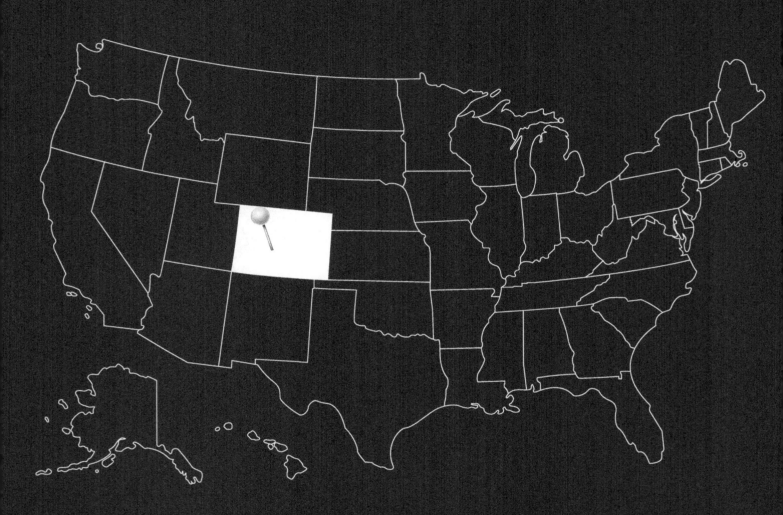

The Rocky Mountains, often called the Rockies, form the largest mountain range in North America, stretching over 3,000 miles from Canada down to New Mexico in the United States.

# Connecticut
## Litchfield Hills

The Litchfield Hills region is known for its picturesque landscapes, characterized by rolling hills, charming villages, and historic covered bridges.

# Delaware
## Bombay Hook National Wildlife Refuge

Bombay Hook National Wildlife Refuge is a critical stopover for migrating shorebirds along the Atlantic Flyway. Each year, thousands of birds, including sandpipers and plovers, rest and feed in the refuge's marshes and mudflats during their long journey.

# Florida
## Everglades

Everglades National Park is the largest tropical wilderness of any kind in the United States and is home to a unique ecosystem of sawgrass marshes, mangroves, and freshwater sloughs. One fascinating resident of the Everglades is the American alligator, a keystone species in the park.

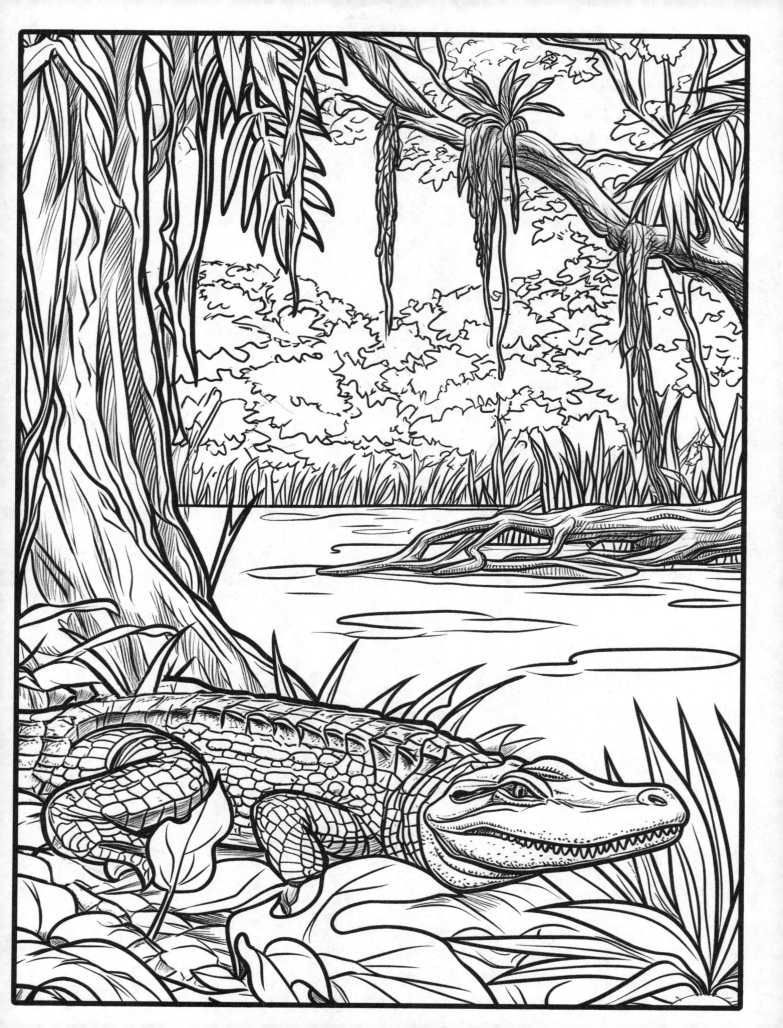

# Georgia
## Savannah's Forsyth Park

Forsyth Park in Savannah, Georgia, is home to the famous Forsyth Fountain, which was inspired by the Place de la Concorde in Paris. The fountain, built in 1858, features multiple tiers and has become an iconic symbol of the city.

# Hawaii
## Nepali Coast

The Napali Coast is renowned for its sheer sea cliffs, some of which rise as high as 4,000 feet from the Pacific Ocean. These cliffs are not only visually stunning but also hold great cultural significance in Hawaiian history and mythology.

# Idaho
## Shoshone Falls

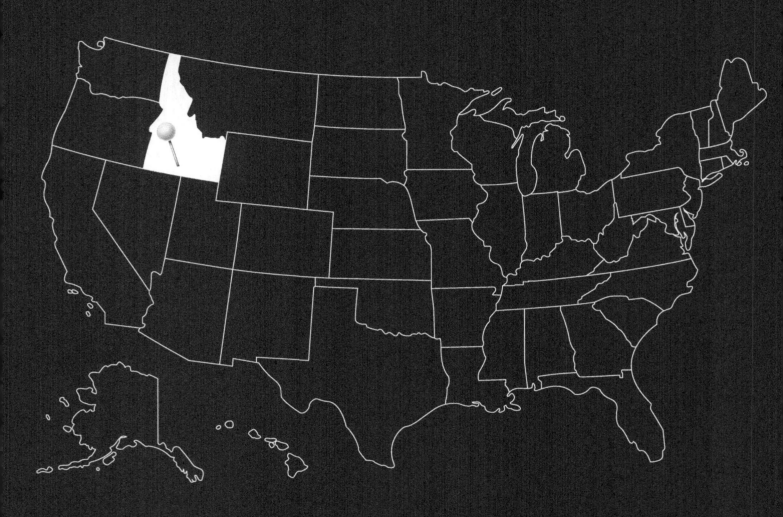

Shoshone Falls, often called the "Niagara of the West," is actually higher than Niagara Falls, measuring 212 feet compared to Niagara's 167 feet. During the spring runoff, the falls can be even more impressive than its eastern counterpart.

# Illinois
## Starved Rock State Park

Starved Rock State Park is home to 18 canyons formed by glacial meltwater and the Illinois River. One of the park's most unique features is its seasonal waterfalls, which flow after heavy rains or during the spring thaw, creating a picturesque scene.

# Indiana
## Brown County State Park

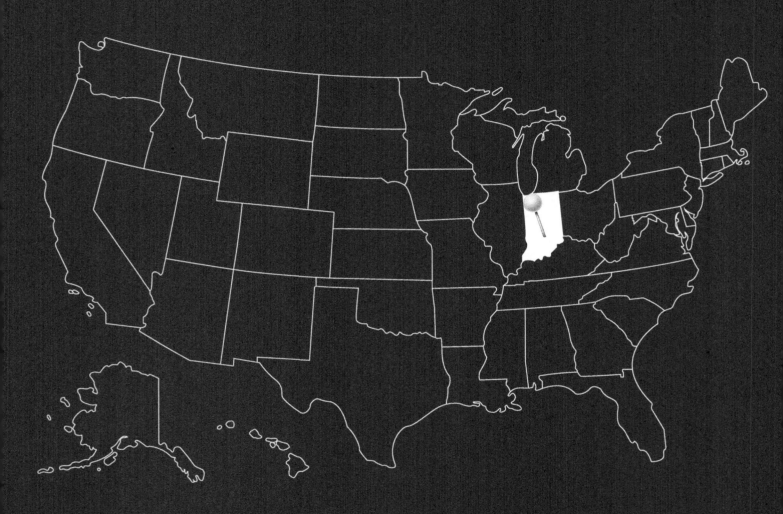

Brown County State Park is often called the "Little Smokies" because of its resemblance to the Great Smoky Mountains. One unique aspect of the park is its fire tower, which visitors can climb for panoramic views of the surrounding hills and forests.

# Iowa
## Loess Hills

The Loess Hills are made up of wind-blown soil deposits called loess, which were formed during the last Ice Age. These unique hills are recognized as one of the most extensive deposits of loess in the world, providing a distinct landscape in the midst of the Midwest.

# Kansas
## Flint Hills

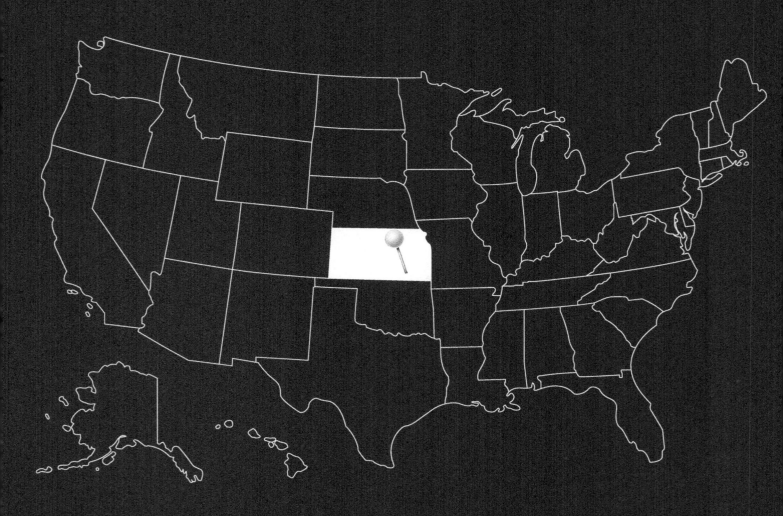

The Flint Hills are not only known for their sweeping grasslands but also for their role in preserving a vanishing ecosystem. These hills are the last remaining tallgrass prairie in North America, making them an important area for conservation efforts.

# Kentucky
## Cumberland Falls

Cumberland Falls is one of the few places in the world where you can witness a moonbow, a rainbow produced by the light of the full moon. This natural phenomenon occurs on clear nights at the base of the falls, creating a magical and rare sight.

# Louisiana
## Bayou

Louisiana's bayous are home to unique wildlife, including the American alligator and the Louisiana black bear. These waterways also serve as important cultural and economic hubs for Louisiana, with Cajun and Creole cultures flourishing along the bayous.

# Maine
## Acadia National Park

Thunder Hole is a popular attraction in Acadia where waves crash into a narrow inlet, creating a thunderous sound. Visitors can witness the power of the ocean as waves shoot upward, sometimes reaching heights of 40 feet.

# Maryland
## Assateague Island

Assateague Island is known for its population of wild horses, believed to have descended from domesticated horses that survived a shipwreck off the coast centuries ago. These horses have adapted to the island's environment and are a beloved sight to behold.

# Massachusetts
## Cape Cod

Cape Cod is a premier destination for whale watching, with opportunities to spot humpback whales, fin whales, and minke whales off its shores. The Stellwagen Bank National Marine Sanctuary, located nearby, is a prime feeding ground for these majestic creatures.

# Michigan
## Pictured Rocks National Lakeshore

Pictured Rocks National Lakeshore is known for its vibrant sandstone cliffs, which get their colors from minerals like copper, iron, and manganese. The cliffs are constantly changing due to erosion, creating a dynamic and ever-evolving landscape.

# Minnesota
## Boundary Waters

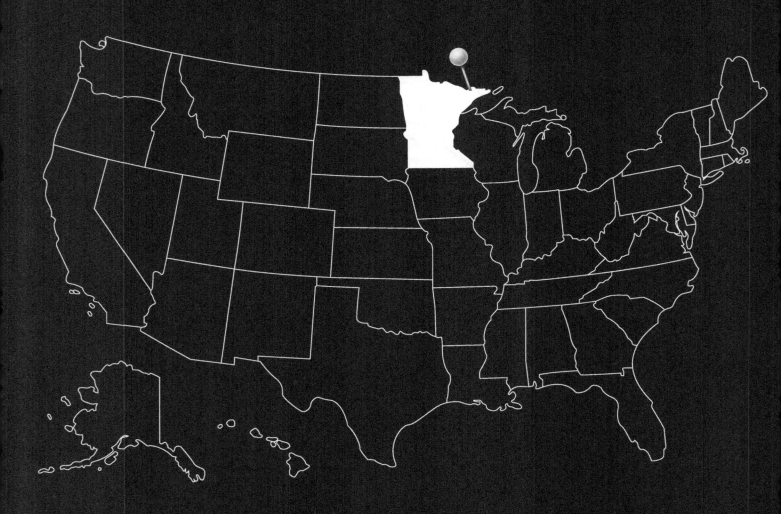

The Boundary Waters Canoe Area Wilderness contains over 1,000 lakes and 1,200 miles of canoe routes, making it one of the most popular wilderness areas for canoeing in the United States. What makes it unique is its strict regulations on motorized boats, preserving the area's pristine and tranquil environment.

# Mississippi
## Natchez State Parkway

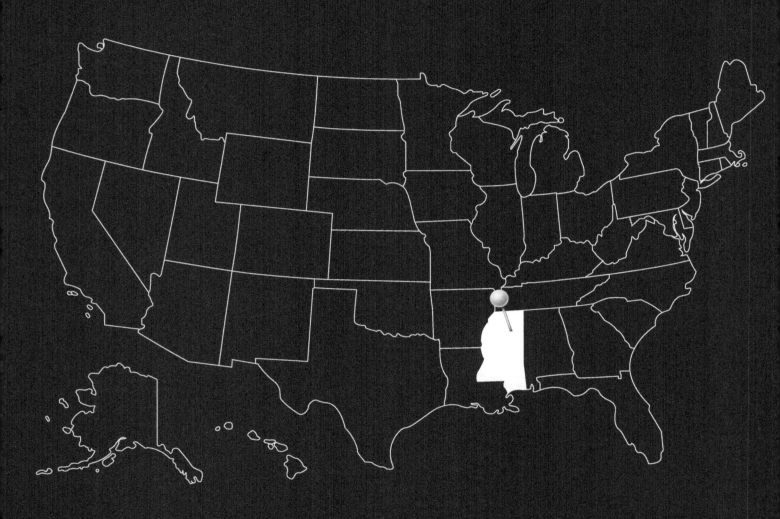

The Natchez Trace Parkway follows a historic trail that was used by Native Americans and later by European settlers, creating a living history corridor. Today, visitors can drive the parkway and explore numerous historic sites, including Native American mounds and Civil War battlefields.

# Missouri
## Ozark National Scenic Riverways

The Ozark National Scenic Riverways is the first national park area to protect a river system. This unique designation helps preserve the pristine Current and Jacks Fork Rivers, which offer some of the best floating and paddling experiences in the Midwest.

# Montana
## Glacier National Park

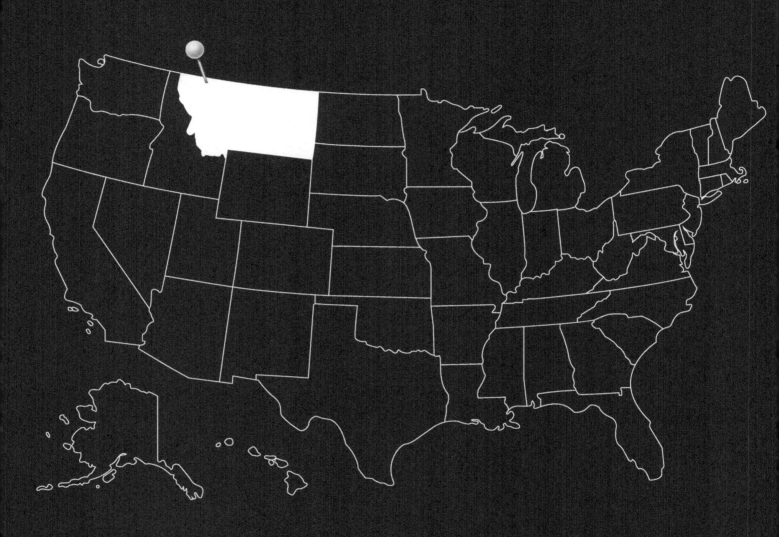

Glacier National Park is home to more than 700 lakes, including Lake McDonald, one of the largest and most picturesque lakes in the park. What makes it unique is that the lake's crystal-clear waters are fed by glaciers, giving it a stunning turquoise hue.

# Nebraska
## Sandhill Wetlands

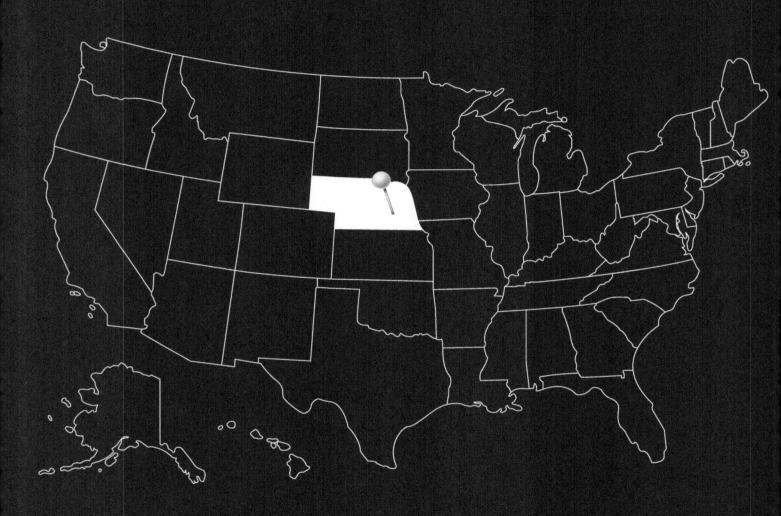

The wetlands are part of the largest remaining wetland complex in the central United States, covering over 3.5 million acres. This diverse ecosystem includes marshes, lakes, rivers, and grasslands, providing habitat for a wide variety of plant and animal species.

# Nevada
## Valley of Fire State Park

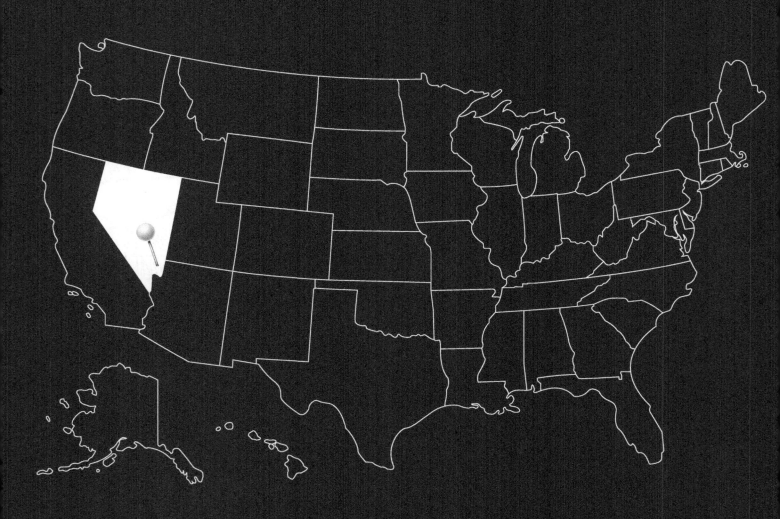

Valley of Fire State Park is home to ancient petroglyphs created by Native Americans thousands of years ago. These intricate rock carvings depict scenes of daily life, wildlife, and spiritual beliefs of the ancient inhabitants of the region.

# New Hampshire
## White Mountains

New Hampshire's White Mountains are home to the Mount Washington Observatory, one of the oldest weather observatories in the United States. This observatory sits atop Mount Washington, known for some of the most extreme weather conditions on Earth, including hurricane-force winds.

# New Jersey
## Great Swamp National Wildlife Refuge

The Great Swamp National Wildlife Refuge is designated as an Important Bird Area, providing crucial habitat for over 240 bird species, including migratory birds like the great blue heron and the colorful wood duck.

# New Mexico
## White Sands National Park

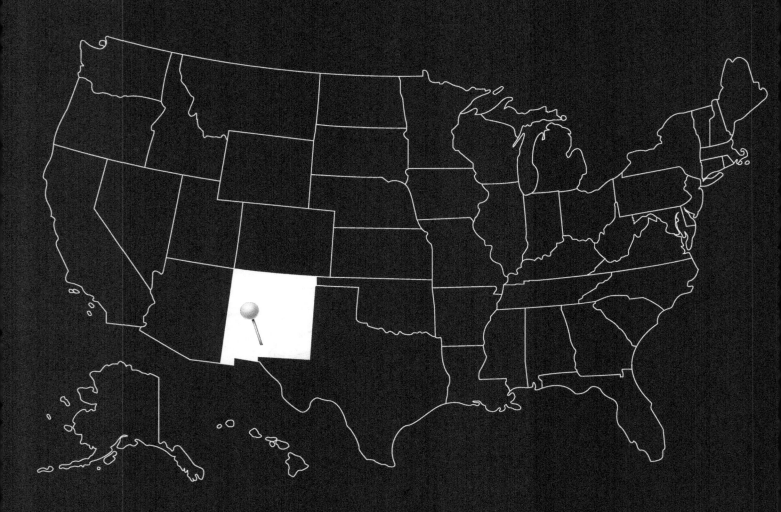

White Sands National Park is home to the largest gypsum dunefield in the world, covering 275 square miles. What makes it unique is that the gypsum sand reflects sunlight, giving the dunes a brilliant white appearance that is unlike any other desert landscape.

# New York
## Adirondack Mountains

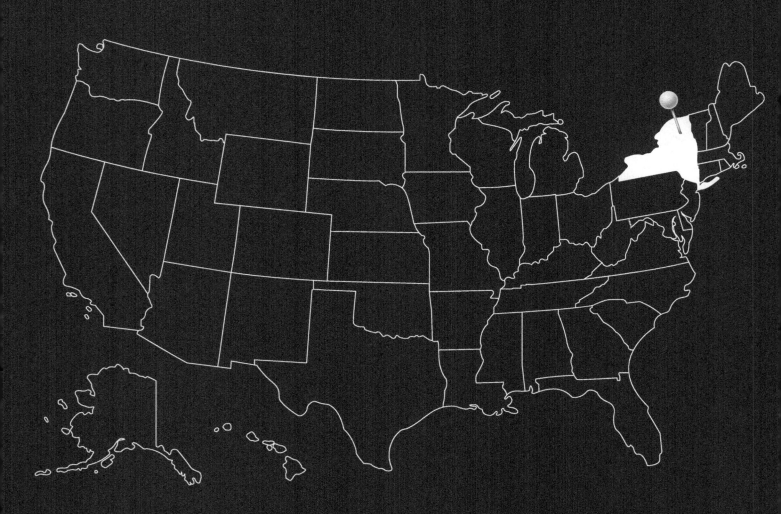

New York's Adirondack Mountains are home to the High Peaks Wilderness Area, which contains 46 peaks over 4,000 feet in elevation. One unique aspect is that becoming an Adirondack 46er, someone who has climbed all 46 peaks, is a popular and prestigious achievement among hikers.

# North Carolina
## Blue Ridge Parkway

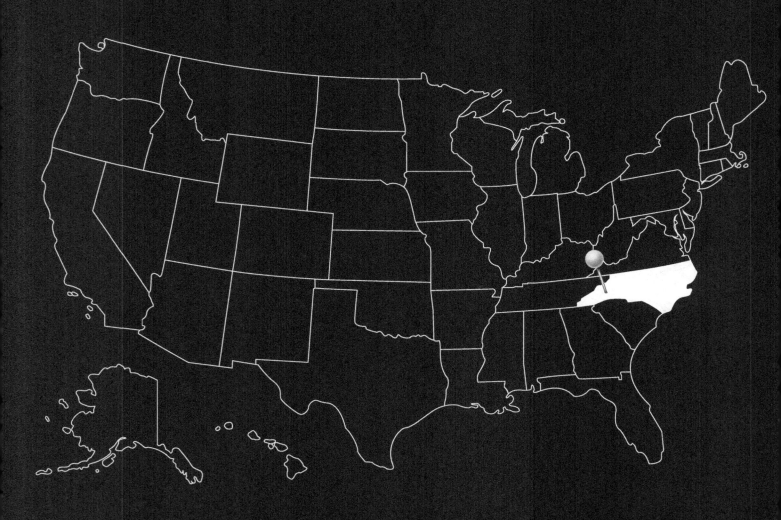

The Blue Ridge Parkway is a scenic road stretching 469 miles through the Blue Ridge
Mountains, offering breathtaking views of rolling hills, forests, and valleys.

# North Carolina
## Blue Ridge Parkway

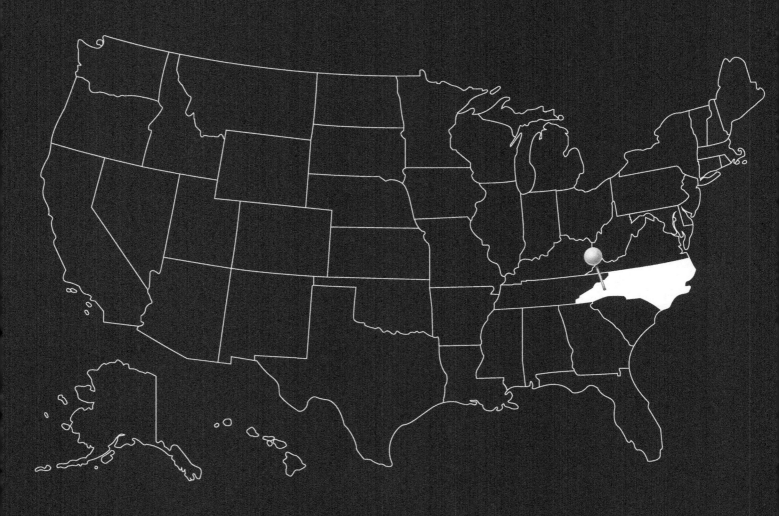

At its highest point, the Blue Ridge Parkway reaches an elevation of 6,053 feet at Richland Balsam, making it the highest paved road in the eastern United States.

# North Dakota
## Theodore Roosevelt National Park

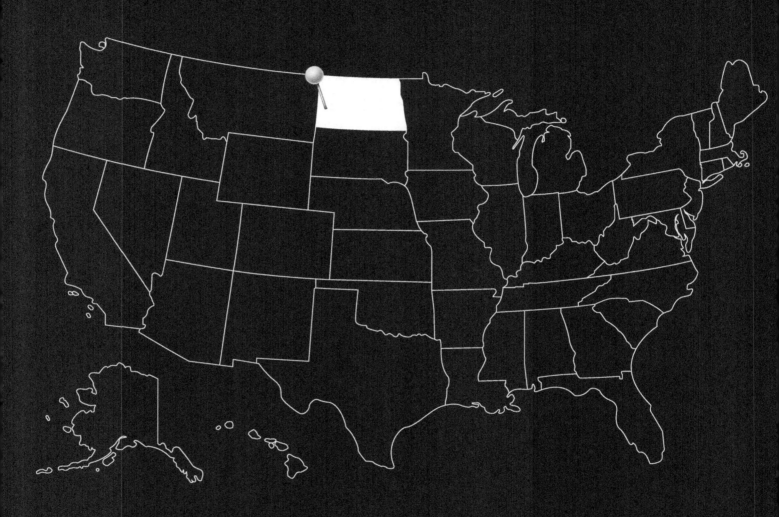

Theodore Roosevelt National Park is named after the 26th president of the United States, who credited his time in the badlands of North Dakota with shaping his conservation ethic. The park preserves not only the landscape but also Roosevelt's legacy as a conservationist.

# Ohio
## Hocking Hills State Park

Hocking Hills State Park is home to Ash Cave, one of the largest recess caves in the state. What makes it unique is that during the summer solstice, the sun sets directly through the opening of the cave, creating a stunning natural spectacle.

# Oklahoma
## Wichita Mountains Wildlife Refuge

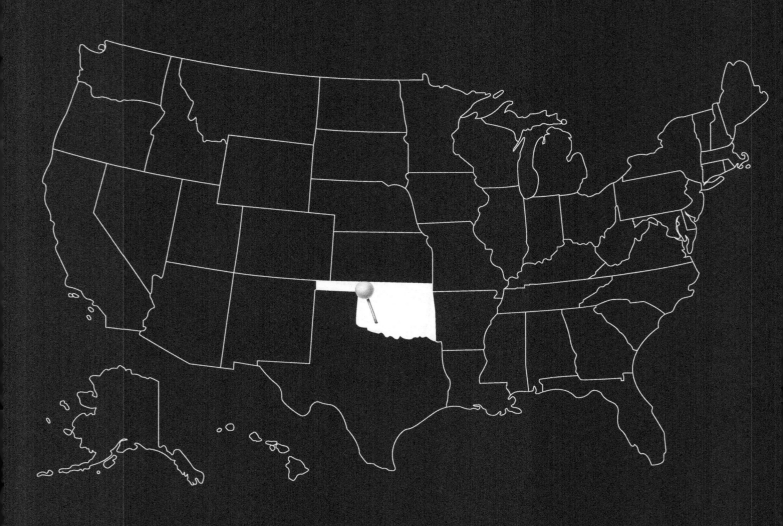

Oklahoma's Wichita Mountains Wildlife Refuge is home to a herd of American bison that roam freely within the refuge. Visitors can often see these majestic animals grazing on the prairie, providing a glimpse into the state's natural heritage.

# Oregon
## Crater Lake

Crater Lake is the deepest lake in the United States, with a maximum depth of 1,943 feet. What makes it unique is that the lake's intense blue color is due to its incredible depth and purity, making it one of the clearest lakes in the world.

# Pennsylvania
## Ricketts Glen State Park

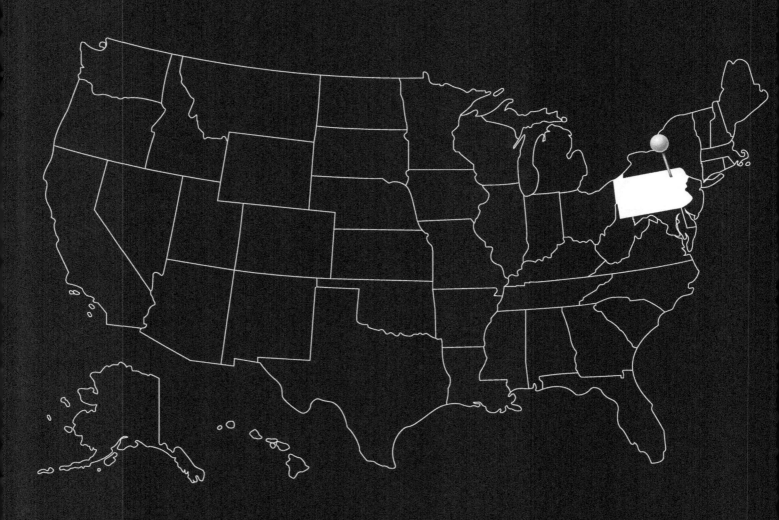

Ricketts Glen State Park is home to Ganoga Falls, the tallest waterfall in the park at 94 feet. What makes it unique is that the falls are part of a series of 24 named waterfalls along Kitchen Creek, making it a paradise for waterfall enthusiasts.

# Rhode Island
## Narragansett Bay

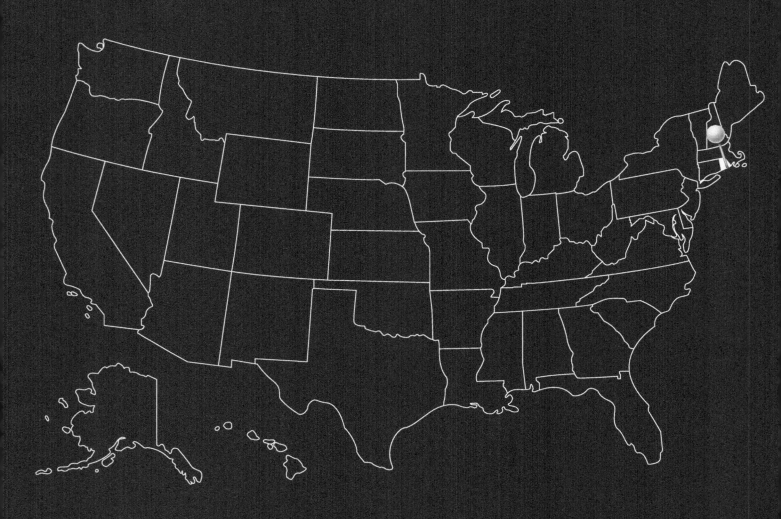

Narragansett Bay is home to the Newport Cliff Walk, a 3.5-mile trail that winds along the rocky coastline. What makes it unique is that the trail passes by some of the Gilded Age mansions of Newport, offering a glimpse into the opulent history of the area.

# Rhode Island
## Narragansett Bay

Narragansett Bay has served as a bustling hub of maritime commerce since the early days of the colony. In the 18th and 19th centuries, the bay was a center for shipbuilding, with numerous shipyards dotting its shores. Vessels built in these shipyards sailed the waters of the bay and beyond, contributing to Rhode Island's reputation as a maritime powerhouse. Today, remnants of this maritime history can still be seen in the historic waterfronts and lighthouses that line Narragansett Bay, offering a glimpse into its rich seafaring past.

# South Carolina
## Congaree National Park

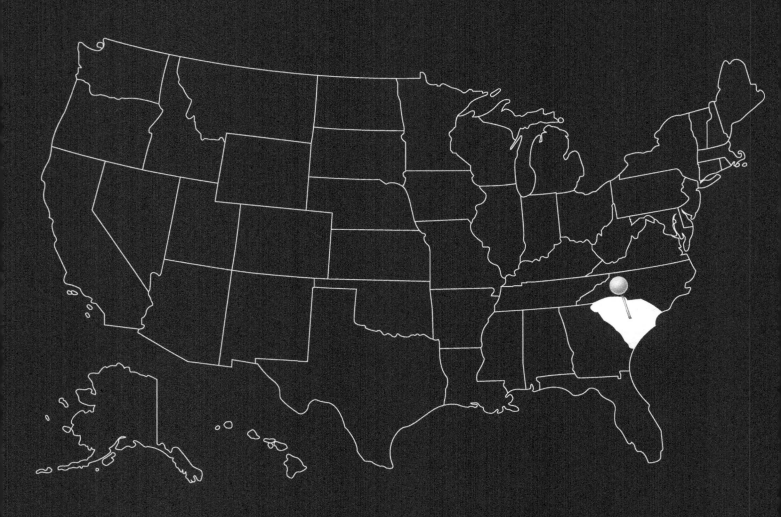

Congaree National Park is home to some of the tallest trees in the eastern United States, including massive bald cypress and loblolly pine trees. What makes it unique is that the park protects one of the last remaining old-growth bottomland hardwood forests in the country.

# South Dakota
## Mount Rushmore

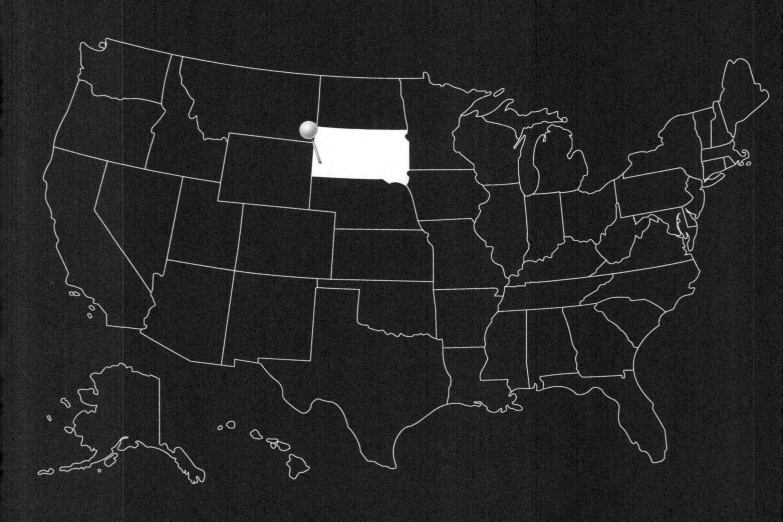

Mount Rushmore was originally conceived as a way to promote tourism in the Black Hills region. The faces of George Washington, Thomas Jefferson, Theodore Roosevelt, and Abraham Lincoln were chosen to represent the nation's birth, growth, development, and preservation, respectively.

# Tennessee
## Great Smoky Mountains

The Great Smoky Mountains National Park is one of the few places in the United States where synchronous fireflies can be seen. These fireflies, which flash their lights in unison during mating season, create a magical and rare natural spectacle.

# Texas
## Big Bend National Park

Big Bend National Park is one of the least light-polluted areas in the United States, making it a prime location for stargazing. What makes it unique is that the park is designated as an International Dark Sky Park, offering unparalleled views of the night sky.

# Utah
## Arches National Park

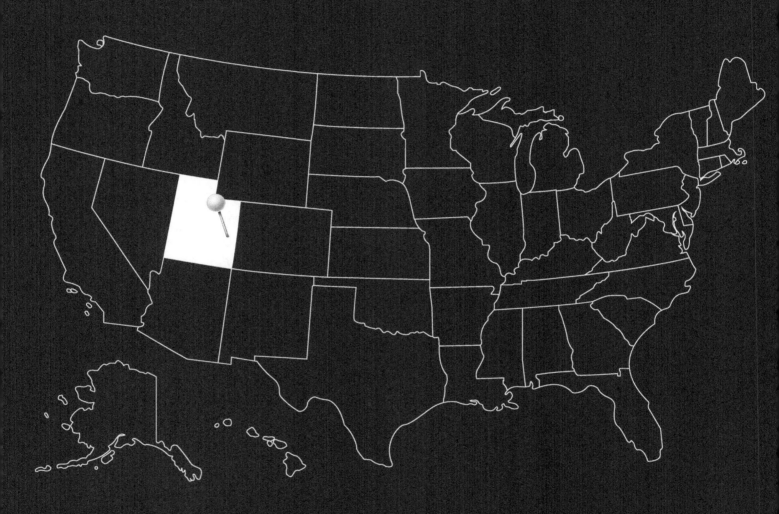

Arches National Park in Utah is home to Delicate Arch, one of the most iconic and photographed arches in the world. What makes it unique is that it is a freestanding natural arch, meaning it is not attached to any cliff or wall.

# Vermont
## Maple Syrup Farm

Vermont's maple syrup industry produces over one million gallons of maple syrup each year, making it the largest producer in the United States. What makes it unique is that Vermont's sugar maples are tapped for sap during the spring sugaring season, a tradition that dates back centuries.

# Vermont
## Maple Syrup Farm

Vermont takes its maple syrup so seriously that it has strict regulations and grading standards for its syrup. What makes it unique is that Vermont Maple Syrup is classified into four grades: Golden Color with Delicate Taste (formerly Grade A Light Amber), Amber Color with Rich Taste (formerly Grade A Medium Amber), Dark Color with Robust Taste (formerly Grade A Dark Amber), and Very Dark Color with Strong Taste (formerly Grade B). These grades are based on the color and flavor profile of the syrup, with each grade having its own distinct characteristics. Vermont's commitment to quality and consistency has made its maple syrup sought after by connoisseurs around the world.

# Virginia
## Shenandoah National Park

Shenandoah National Park is home to more than 100 miles of the Appalachian Trail, a world-renowned hiking trail that stretches over 2,000 miles from Georgia to Maine. What makes it unique is that the park offers some of the most scenic and accessible sections of the trail.

# Washington
## Olympic National Park

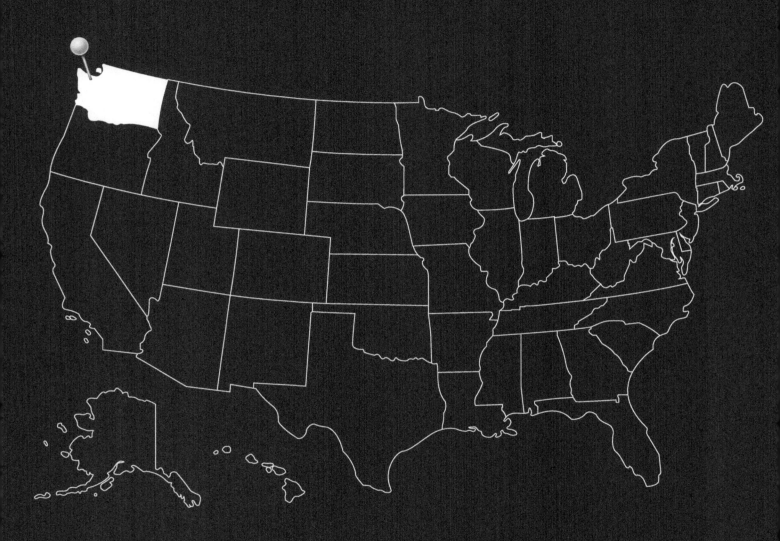

Olympic National Park is home to one of the largest temperate rainforests in the United States. What makes it unique is that this rainforest, known as the Hoh Rainforest, receives an average of 12 to 14 feet of rain each year, creating a lush and vibrant ecosystem.

# West Virgina
## New River Gorge

The New River Gorge Bridge is one of the longest steel arch bridges in the world and is an iconic symbol of the state. What makes it unique is that each October, the bridge serves as the centerpiece for Bridge Day, an extreme sports event where BASE jumpers leap from the bridge into the gorge below.

# Wisconsin
## Door County

Door County is often called the "Cape Cod of the Midwest" for its charming coastal towns and scenic beauty. What makes it unique is that the peninsula is dotted with over 250 miles of shoreline, providing ample opportunities for sailing, kayaking, and enjoying the waterfront.

# Wyoming
## Yellowstone National Park

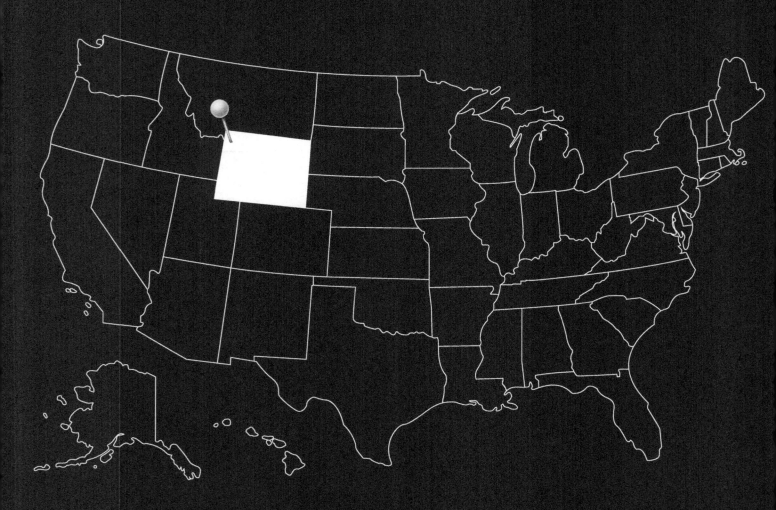

Yellowstone National Park is the world's first national park, established in 1872. It sits atop one of the largest active super volcanoes on the continent. The park is home to more than 10,000 geothermal features, including geysers, hot springs, and bubbling mud pots. One of its most famous geysers, Old Faithful, erupts approximately every 90 minutes, shooting boiling water up to 180 feet into the air. Yellowstone's geothermal wonders and diverse wildlife, including bison, bears, and wolves, make it a truly remarkable and geologically active wilderness.

# Thank You

We hope you enjoyed this unique journey. Please consider leaving us a review by scanning the QR code below. It takes 5 seconds and helps small businesses like ours continue to learn and grow.

▶ Scan for Amazon Review

We also invite you to continue your creative journey by visiting our author site to discover new and upcoming releases.

▶ Scan & discover new releases!